THE
TEN THOUSANDTH
NIGHT

The Ten Thousandth Night

Gwen Head

University of Pittsburgh Press

Published by the University of Pittsburgh Press, Pittsburgh, Pa. 15260
Copyright © 1979, Gwen Head
All rights reserved
Feffer and Simons, Inc., London
Manufactured in the United States of America

Library of Congress Cataloging in Publication Data

Head, Gwen, 1940–
   The ten thousandth night.

  (Pitt poetry series)
   I. Title.
PS3558.E14T4   811'.5'4   78-21991
ISBN 0-8229-3391-8
ISBN 0-8229-5301-3 pbk.

Many of these poems have appeared in *Calyx, Chowder Review, Iron Country, The Niagara Magazine, Poetry Northwest, Poetry NOW, Prairie Schooner,* and *Seattle Review.* "First Blood" was originally published in *Concerning Poetry,* © 1978 by Gwen Head. "Not Sleeping" first appeared in *Poetry.* "Coming Down" first appeared in *Poetry*°*Texas,* Vol. 1, Number 2. "Albino Rainbows" first appeared in *Portland Review.*

*The publication of this book is supported
by a grant from the National Endowment for the Arts
in Washington, D.C., a Federal agency.*

In memory of
MARVIN MC GEE
November 11, 1910 – March 28, 1978
and
for my only
LEE
with love and hope

CONTENTS

THE
TEN THOUSANDTH
NIGHT

THE WOMAN IN THE MIDDLE

Begin with the heroine standing on a staircase,
three yards of tapered rose point slung from her shoulders,
in mandatory pearls, stephanotis,
and baby's breath, poised like a white bat.

Above her silken knees, the satin hem
hangs like a blade. It's nineteen twenty-nine.
In steamer trunks beneath the porte cochere,
the trousseau purchased on her grand tour.
Patou: a blue brocade with silver lace,
its bugle beads like regimented rain.
Embroidered black and white Chinese pajamas
to wear in the evenings, playing dominoes.
Teddies and step-ins, ostrich fans. To read,
Tristram and *Sonnets to a Red-Haired Lady*.
To flirt with, a long cigarette holder of
the first green plastic made to look like jade.
His gifts, by which we know across the years
that the groom is poor, but has a good heart.

Twenty-five years later his heart has given out.
Their daughter (a menopausal accident)
is old enough to count him up the stairs.
In steel-rimmed glasses, braces on her teeth,
her busy cranium's wired like a champagne cork.
One, two, three, . . . at ten, another step.
Her scrawny shoulder blades protrude like wings.

The heroine listens, rises — no, it can't be!
Hose at the knees, flesh at the waist, hair
at the nape all rolled and tied or netted down,
and all an anonymous, shabby package color,
all with the slack sway and thump of the sleeper berth.

3

Can't be, but is.
                    This is her dressing table:
desk calendar with six weeks left unturned,
rings of spilt powder, piles of unanswered letters,
and a sealed bottle of Je Reviens.
Stabbing the pins into her hair, she goes
to thread a needle for her dragon mother.

What happens in the middle? Mother, tell me!
I'm in the middle now. Why wasn't there
a lover and a train to throw herself under,
in a last display of the pyrotechnic hair?

Or is this the train, this slow freight of years,
these sodden comforts of the hobo jungle?

LIFE MASK

I

Only my face takes the plunge,
smeared with a channel swimmer's grease.
Long pig, I am served up on a trestle.

"We need your chin up."
I am given a roll of toilet paper for a neck pillow.
The single-handed applause
of the batter bowl rewards me.

"You'll feel some heat at first."
Now I am poured and spatulaed.
Yeastily I bubble through my nose hole
while the weight of plaster lies, smoothing me out.
Eyes clenched, lips taut, I wait
for the cold kiss of permanence.

It comes. The mask sucks and pops, pulling away.
I'm the first pickle from a fresh jar.
Watched over by ceramic trolls, I rise
from my hard bed, postoperative,
and try my earth legs, ashy
with the dust of making.

II

"— the longest eyelashes —"
Fossils, they have embedded themselves in plaster,
meshed rows of bulrushes,
the eyeballs hidden baskets.

The sculptress tosses clay like pizza dough.
Earthy, aqueous, willful, her medium
slides down the nose chute,
stagnates in eye sockets.

5

Into the sterile furrow of the lips
the clay is tamped, patted, smoothed.
Between press and probing hand, a semblance
of flesh takes shape.
The packed mold is inscrutable as a thunder egg.

Meanwhile, behind the monocular
turret of her camera, the model
prowls, shooting. A nameless gray day
eyes her through the skylight.
Leaving, she will commend
this dream to the furnace: a self
all congealed flame, crystalline,
jagged.

III

The box says "pure old-fashioned peanut butter."
Inside, two lumpish versions of myself.
One is a somnambulist whose broken eyes
stare beneath stone awnings from an unclimbable tower.
The almost-recognizable other, prognathous,
takes things as they come, on the chin.
Her hair is rendered in rubbery bathing cap waves.
Grimacing, she surfaces again, eyes gritted shut,
themselves the jaws of traps behind which
some endless secret gnawing toward freedom occurs.

And indeed the smell of the thing when I lift and hold it
is unbearable: acrid, metallic,
a taint of dried blood.

QUEEN CONCHES

For Allan

You and I strolled by the sea.
The offshore scrims of sunset
rustled meekly into place.
The sand was studded with conch shells,
cabbage-sized, bony parodies of the clouds.
You picked one up.
It was knobby, moist, foolishly
pink, the skull of a newborn,
only one small chink
an unclosed fontanel
above the chubby protrusions.
We, I have forgotten to mention,
were lovely, sensual, younger,
anointed with sunblock and insect repellent.

Of course we took it home with us,
strumpet shell, trollop shell, replica
of Balzac's boudoir,
its stone damasks and cashmeres
spread always in welcome.
Little horns, ravished operculum,
pouting, pearly nether lip:
we relegated it, and rightly,
to the bedroom.

There is another shell where I work,
the gift of a charter boat skipper down on his luck.
All its cotton candy is eaten away,
its silken floss spun out.
What remains is a conspiracy
of little windows that scatter the light into lace.
What remains is the sea
itself in a winding sheet,

and over it corals
lift shattered candelabra.
What remains is a hard-bitten diagram
of ruin, its spiral an ever-
evolving, ever-enlarging cul de sac.
This shape fits my hand like a weapon.

A naturalist might note
that shells are exoskeletons;
a moralist, that both of my shells
began as shelter.

STINGING NETTLE

Its disguise resides in the commonplace.
The ancient shabby needle of the fields
plies its trade among blackberries, under dock,
or apes the sprawling pungency of mint.
Stalks upright, leaves opposite, toothed, of an attenuated
heart shape, its flowers loll in pendulous racemes
so little showy they seem an irritant,
like lint or a fallen eyelash.
Dioica, incomplete, of one sex only,
they inhabit, like Godwin and Wollstonecraft, two houses
to express the furious rectitude of their separateness.

You know the rest. Under the microscope
the leaves and stems bristle
with narrow metallic volcanoes.
Brushed, they erupt in poison, invisible, adamant
as unrequited love;
                                        but should you, in rage
and pain, crush the offending
branch, the blood of the nettle will surely heal you,
just as, scalded, the spiteful shoots
turn tame and nourishing.
                                        Further, the caterpillar
of the ravishing Admiral Skipper
feeds only on stinging nettle; and perhaps the butterflies
too are immune, and return
each summer in frivolous flight like love letters
among the stern catkins.

One final warning. The plant is perennial.
Its roots multiply deep, in hiding.
Its pain, like that of childbirth, is strangely effaceable.
Forgetful, you may grasp it time and again
in an open field, among flowers.

SWEET AMARYLLIS

No amorous giant
could equal the length
that springs from this plain brown bulb
with the wrinkled skin.
Leaving nothing to the imagination
two censorious leaves
point upward from the base

at this tense hammerhead crane
wearing a bonfire of flowers
like a foolish bonnet,
this wildcat windmill, this phallus
decorated not with forget-me-nots
but with sizzling pinwheels.

Androgynous, you wear a nymph's name.
Wallflower, your pot too tight
and shiny for dancing, you lean
in the doorway, sweating nectar,
spilling pollen like face powder.

Half succubus, half angel, attended
by the wizard ginkgo, and the uncanny
monkeypod tree, you appeared
to Linnaeus, wearing nine heads,
each furnished with a serpent's tongue.
Four voices, then, can never be enough
to sing your praises.

Amaryllis, sweet amaryllis!
Still, when you are mute,
let me sing how your long leaves
die back into the bulb
like sputtering fuses; how you lie
all winter in dry earth,
in your scaly heart, white and waiting,
an embryonic armada,
the translucent sails of its flowers
furled like umbrellas;

and how spring after spring you return,
remaking yourself
out of memory.

THE FACTS OF LIFE

For Lee

The body is not on your side.
While you are trying to sleep, or writing a poem
in your head, it shelters the shadiest
activities. In the attic
they show blue movies
and on the ground floor
is an establishment whose interior
is red, dim, plush.

Commotion in the bordello!
The doors swing wide, the walls of the place are shaking.
A mob of customers barges in.
It is clear they are all villains,
so many abstract twitching moustaches,
so many leering eyebrows.
They riot, yet all goes swimmingly.
But one skulks behind the portieres.
He looks for a hidden door.

You would not like the madam.
She is fat. She lolls in an antechamber.
She doesn't come out for the party.
She pouts. The truth is she never
wanted to leave her sisters.
But he finds her magnetic.
He's a plunger. He loses his head.
Spiderlike, she swallows him.
But he doesn't die. They are
beside themselves repeatedly,
chromosomes clinging and cleaving,
genes kissing their doubles.

This goes on for months.
The bordello becomes a machine shop.
It is a growth industry.
Overcrowding ensues.

In another scenario the floozie sulks alone.
It's an off night. The customers
find the atmosphere poisonous.
One or two take a look around
but she isn't there, or she's wearing her hair in curlers.
The place isn't what it used to be.
Trash it! Tear down the curtains,
rip the red paper to shreds,
yank the stuffing out of the pillows.
It all goes out with the garbage.

Each time, you are the informer,
the outraged moralist, the vice squad.
The body? It only wants
to make you happy.

WATER BABIES

The locker room floor
is slippery with banana peels.
Its talcumed air
is the air of a guano island.
From this port the mothers embark,
majestic of beam, tugged
by the young they will shortly cast off.

And now they are the shores of the one continent
from which all histories, great and small,
break loose and drift.
What waves of bawling crash against their ears!
They smile, they croon to the voyagers
who lie thrashing, eyes pinched shut,
in the glassy isolation of water,
a squared-off second amnion in which chlorine
cancels the essential salt.
Fragrant, far, merciless,
the spice islands of origin
step back and back, impregnable
behind the flowering atolls of their bathing dresses.

Still, water connects them, kinked
and pulsing. Mutual wrath
drives the fat pistons, sets
the infantile engines hooting like calliopes.
Theirs is the first fury. Gasping, bellicose,
through breaking waves they rush upon the world.

THE HOUR-GLASS

After Jules Renard

I

Sliding reciprocals,
two airy triangles
outlined in string
grow in and out
of each other, grating hard
at the narrow point
of intersection.
               Mother and child
smiling, lean above
the cat's cradle.
           Love
kills intelligence. The brain and the heart
act on each other
in the manner of an hour-glass.

This is amazing.
Under the soft, curved lips
the slow-motion camera
sees spittle glisten
on bared teeth, observes
the strangler's flex of knuckles
as the fingertips dally and soothe.

One fills itself
only to empty the other.

II

Riding the swing
of wide-set ropes
the two, sweating and spangled,
kick out towards each other.

The world would be happy
if it were upside down.

15

One leaps. They lock wrists,
and, with legs spraddled, fly
across the white spotlight

in a furious x, vote
of no confidence, fracture mark
mapping ways to break stone.

Death is comforting.
It delivers us
from the thought of death.

III

She is a deadly
black jewel with legs.
On her belly, no star,
but two red triangles
joined at the apex.

All the same
little by little
I give up a great many things
that I cannot have.

CIRCE

The wind grinds its teeth. A sleepless moon
floats in a sea of purple lees and whey.
In a snarl of tendril tails and flap ears,
ripe backs bulging like gourds, the pigs wait for their queen.
Their delicate trotters pinch the silken mud
trying its texture. Intelligent and mean
their black eyes swarm over her like aphids.

Bare feet precise as mattocks, she advances
through a meadow blue with chicory and forget-me-nots.
She wears a gown of thin and luminous onionskin.
Her hair is a rumpled cataract of fennel.

Lady of gardens, she offers up her burdens,
lets them devour the shapes they have made their own:
garlands of shaved peel, cushions of pulp, mounds
and ruffles of crisp and moist, the bitter rind
and grimy roots of her being, forked and swollen.

All, down to the shriveled and lethal kernel,
final, adamant, ominous as bone
she tenders her lovers, mistress of sty, kennel,
and lair, sum of her offerings, slut queen.

MARE'S MILK

The Countess Sonya Tolstoy

Fresh from his first cure "I,
aged, toothless fool
that I am, have fallen in love,"
Lyovochka wrote to his aunt.
Declaring himself to me
in cipher, he traced
initials in chalk on my parents' card table.
"Your youth, your thirst for happiness . . ."

I guessed the rest, and knew that I must love him,
and tried, and did.
                    "Her terror. Something morbid.
She knows all."
                    I knew nothing.
"It is impossible" he wrote
"that all this should end except with life itself."

Nine years later "You looked old,
too thin, and pitiful"
he wrote, away for his second cure,
of the picture I had sent.
A kerchief covered my head, shaved bare
when I tossed delirious from childbed fever:
our fifth, a daughter, all still living then.

"My friend, great writer of the Russian land,
return to literature,"
Turgenev, his great friend,
dying, wrote to him.
Gorged on sun, mutton, fermented
mare's milk, worn out with riding, in his skin
tent, did he read, did he answer?

18

Back from Samara, he visits
muzhiks on their deathbeds, rages
when a son plays joyful dances on the piano.
Incurable, he lives his life on paper.
He has no words for death.
He will never answer.

I have written little and badly, interrupted
by children, nursing, noise.
I am ridiculous
in his eyes now, and know it.
Some nights, switching my coarse hair by the embers
alone, I think of the mares and the strong women
who brew their pungent milk in leather sacks.
I see the moonlight stroke their bold flanks,
their proud heads. They bear and nourish all,
never resting. All is distance without them.

They lie down only to die.

EDITH ASCENDING

Veering among the fireflies, two constant lights.
Loud among the cicadas, a harsher rasping.
Only I was awake to see the American lady
and her gentleman friend arrive. Swaddled in white
linen head to toe, wearing goggles in utter darkness,
through billows of dust and moonlight they ascended.
Our sleepy songbirds woke and mistook them for morning.

We offered them anchovies, cheese, oil soup.
Then their driver, even at that hour,
saw to his rubber-shod mount, and stroked its flanks
till they shone again. At last all slept.
                                        But at dawn
she was up, demanding to see our poor child
in his wreath of dusty grapes, and our startled mother
flaking sweetly from the chapel wall. By the gate
the automobile once more stood snorting and fuming,
shy at the edge of the cliff. Its fifty headstrong
horses, it seems, were made only for climbing.

We had no bells that morning. With twenty men
on our end of the borrowed rope, we swung them down,
tolling the slow switchbacks one by one,
till the road eased, the pine boughs resumed their hushed
                                        breathing,
and the strangers were saved. Perhaps all miracles
happen so: sweat, noise, exorbitant demands.
Still such a fall might have had its own beauty.

Often I think of the signora.
Who holds her back now?

EDITH CAST DOWN

Summer afternoon. They lift me at the window
to see my garden grown again. One awful week, years ago,
my cook was flung from his cycle, his neck snapped;
and my footman, poor crazy sympathetic Romano
shot dead by his jealous wife, the local *cocotte*
who, in a word, boiled over.
Then came the sudden wind, wrenching and tearing,
that filled the parterre between the boxwood hedges
with a potpourri of salad greens and roses
and left my cut-leaf maples both dismasted.
At dinner that night, there was an unseemly pause
between the entree and the roast: the second cook
lay senseless in his blood on the kitchen floor,
an eel seethed in red wine. I was not, of course,
informed until after the brandy. All that is seven
years ago already. New maples sway in my window.
They close the blinds. I am lifted to bed again.
My hand moves in a foolish benediction.

"So here it is at last, the distinguished thing."
He was deceived, my dear Henry. For two months
the unworldly stranger loitered on his threshhold
and each long day he was lifted, as I am,
to his window, to watch the ships toylike and far
on the sullen Thames, and the white fog coming.
La pensée ne meurt pas . . . can that be true?
Thank God we never wasted him, not then,
not now, though he is gone twenty years.
In the buzzing heat my cypress rock at anchor,
my mists are of lavender. How long
after all have I been dying? I loathe
this undistinguished lingering. No window
can ever open wide enough. I want
the limitless spaces.

21

NOT SLEEPING

It is always too cold or too hot.
Like docile servants bearing
late mail, cold tea, the little
ills of the body announce themselves
and are naggingly present, friendly
when you would have them silent. Meanwhile
your mind plays all the wrong records, and a far
gate bangs in the wind.

In any house there are rooms for not sleeping.
Wakeful, you can do almost anything:
wax the floor until it gleams like a skating rink,
pay your bills, evolve a philosophy,
eat all the leftovers, water your plants, contemplate
the worsening world situation.
Unless you live alone, no music
except what you can read silently from score,
though if light-footed you may dance a little
or look in on your loved ones sleeping.

If these fail, move on.
Take a long drive, tracing the line
of some coast or other. Find
a new town, a late bar, a stranger's
bed, in which to lie wakeful
while far off some balky engine chugs and whines
and the gate goes on banging in your mind.

Still, courage. Nothing is more certain
than that, whether by stealth or by force
with or without your knowledge and consent
when you most expect it
when you least expect it
whether you think it is time or no
the wind will subside
the gate flop shut like a hymnal

and sleep will come.

DREAD

In Muybridge's world, each creature
biped or quadruped
runs its single course unimpeded.
Clocked, segmented,
the frames slap into place:
railroad ties or a game of patience.

Actions flow out of each other.
The future bursts
from the ruptured cell wall.
Each motion, ambling or violent
unfolds, ebbs, returns
in the simple tripartite pattern
of songs or flowers.
And the light is so spacious, so ripe.
Moving cornucopias, still lives
of globe and piston, toothsome,
ramshackle, spill from these pages.

The dog grins,
tongue slack in the spanking breeze.
The eagle splashes black feathers over graph paper.
The elephant's loose skin flows and sparkles.
We forget that lives collide.
We forget those not running are fighting.

One card is always missing.
The locomotive bears down.
A hidden cell detonates and goes dark.

A melody lies asphyxiated on the page,
wings flattened, pins through the thorax.

Somewhere a young man weeps, embracing his wife.
Somewhere a dog springs gaily.
The witty hinges and pivots
of his jaws sweep and gnash,
and a cat shreds into gobbets of bloody flesh.

Her furious hackles drift and settle like thistledown.
And somewhere my hand traces
these words, warding off
the points and shears
that with each frame draw closer.

FIRST BLOOD

Though I speak with the tongues
of men and of angels

> We perched like starlings
> on a grid of folding
> chairs in the gymnasium.

I am become as sounding brass
or tinkling cymbals

> After the reading
> before the hymn
> we were told the news.

A mighty fortress is our God

> As we sang all heads
> turned to your empty seat
> its flimsy metal
> provisional, apologetic,

A bulwark never failing

> and it was as if
> you had won a prize.

— equal to the sum
of the squares of the two sides

> The radiators squealed and farted.
> On each divider
> of my notebook I drew
> a fluent, many-tendriled cartouche
> enclosing nothing.

"You're noan so far
fro' Thornfield now"

26

All day in my mind the door
of your familiar comfortable house
opened and shut like the jaws
of the whale.

No grandeur to overwhelm
no stateliness to embarrass

Under the chapped skin
of my cold hands
subterranean rivers
of blood were flowing.

Nox est perpetua una dormienda
The seconds spattered down like sleet.

Deinde centum, dein mille altera
Your young father below ground by nightfall.

FLOWERING QUINCE

Numb and brown
the branches catch in my doorway
painful as a hangnail,

a snarled net
in which three round
green leaves lie gasping.

Angular, reaching;
what river
has such fractures and interruptions,
such stiff-necked tributaries?

Among them, silk knots,
small cabbages, rabbits' feet
in pawnshop threes,

green breasts with white nipples,
feathered sugar bowls,

fat craters
into which the funicular worm
descends, swaying.

COMING DOWN

The Panhandle landscape near Amarillo, Texas

The wagons came.
The grass fell away from their wheels,
but the ruts stayed.
The ruts have lasted for years.
From the air the ruts shine white on the brown crosshatching
of the fields, the initials of lost
lovers ingrown in bark.
Where the fields peter out
there is lichen and dying moss, its whorls and filaments
canyon and dry wash seen small, and in the canyons
the frail trees bend their shoulders to the wind
that harrows the high plain now, that harrowed it then,
when the first wheels came.

The wheels are spinning.
The wheels are spinning still.
Two days out of sixty, glistening needles of water
eke out their meager circles. Hopeful grass
springs up beneath. Rows of green gauges
record the pressure of growth. Too soon the needles
waver and fall dry.
But the pumps still beat.
With tireless levers and pinions
they alight in the wake of a plenty receding, receding
and day and night utter their scavenger cries.

The wagons have gone.
But all tracks stay and weather
as the bones of an old skull
emerge from the failing flesh.
So now the green gauges darken, the pressure plummets, the
        plundered vaults
of dolomite empty and echo,
and the hot heart of the earth shrinks in on itself,

and the earth wears its flayed skin smiling, brown and downy
as any child's cheek.

The airplane's shadow scissors and glides to rest.
Before me a door opens
into this garden,
this paradise.

VAYA CON DIOS

Buenas tardes, señoras y señores. This is your captain
Raul. *Bienvenidos a Aérolíneas
del Sangre de Cristo, S.A.*
This plane of historical interest
was my father's (may God rest his soul)
and his father's before him.
En nuestro DC 3 Super Clipper, we are flying *ahora*
from Cabo San Lucas to La Paz.
You will notice the seats all face backward.
Our stewardess Father José
will assist upon takeoff.
When he says "May God have mercy
on your souls," we ask that you all exhale
and observe the No Smoking sign.

We will cruise at an altitude of one hundred feet.
Our cabin is not pressurized. The circular objects
on the edge of the luggage racks
are electric fans, not prayer wheels.
There is no emergency exit.
We will soon serve complimentary Holy Communion.

I call your attention to the following points of interest:
on your left, a school of large sharks,
and some pelicans just above the plane.
Look quickly before they pass us.
Please tell our crew if you have any last requests,
and remember our airline's slogan, *Vaya con Dios.*

RECENT ACQUISITIONS

Item: one tea bowl, Japanese *Oribe*
of a frozen porridge color
its rim marked
by three vertical lines
terminating in circular scrawls.
These may be read
  as spiders
  amulets, arrested
  raindrops
  plummeting
into a deep green glaze whose color suggests
  if organic, dragonflies
  if chemical, arsenic.

Item: *Conus*
aulicus, reticulated
black and white shell of the Philippine tide line.
On its curved obsidian
sides, a perspective
of large and small white cones
erupts, an infant mountain range extruded
from the obscure sea floor.

Item: on the leathery
moss and cream-colored foliage
of *Paphiopedilum concolor*
a similar pattern
recurs, a softened and flutelike
canon at the octave;
but its bloom, while of an appealing
lavender-speckled yellow
is sparse, infrequent, and for an orchid, totally
insignificant.

Finally, on a still-cryptic
curl of ghostly gelatin
in a metal can, this snapshot:
    framed
        by yellowing Royal palms
    left
        green-shingled Colonial
        "ADAMS FUNERAL HOME"
    center
        low-lying, white, s-curved, voluptuous,
        "A Morris Lapidus Associates Renovation,
        HEAVEN"
    foreground
        the choppy brown canal
        one heedless pleasure boat
        a third sign
        "WATCH YOUR WAKE."

MANTA RAYS

Kaupulehu, Kona, Hawaii

Night after night
on the same circuit
they come, cruising the shallows,
the shadows, haunted by plankton,
to the soft swish and lull
of water beneath this floodlight.

Binocular to excess
their eyes look away from each other,
duelists who have paced off their distance
and now stand back to back
preparing to fire.

The rest of their heads is all mouth.
Like immense sugar tongs
lined with silver and pearl
two cartilaginous mandibles
clasp the water
we see as vacant.

In feathery washes
of ink and blurred charcoal
they bear on their broad backs
the nocturnal markings
of moth or barn swallow.
Yet their bellies are all noon and sand.
And their tails, vestigial afterthoughts,
whisper *quirt, stiletto, shiv,*
wounding the yielding swell.

Dark sails that the water enters,
fills, and propels,
they swim, straining light.
Their bodies are all undulation:
rolling, unrolling
white boneless wing tips
against the porous rocks
like rug merchants displaying their wares,
or, in the black distance, setting
pale triangles flapping like storm warnings.

What invisible lines
hold them tethered here, weaving
on the heavy current,
wet kites
rubber seraphim
for whom moving, feeding, breathing
are one?

SLUG

How can he dare to cross me,
this oozing footless tube,
lifting his alert pronged head
in the cuckold's gesture?

Long ago his nation
cast off the security of shells
and now go proudly naked
relying for safety
on the *realpolitik*
of sheer slug numbers.

Clearly he glories
in each nuance of slug calligraphy,
those sly paths of silver
that chronicle the progress
of appetite, and answer
the urgent appeals of the rain.

Perhaps he incarnates
the slug king of legend
who lay for seven days and seven nights
besotted in a saucer of beer
but did not drown

and who, by this test
won his dappled queen
and with her dangled upside down
on a glittering rope
of commingled slime
convulsed and tranquil
as a hypnotist's pendulum.

Then together they passed
through the exorcist's circles
of slug bait unharmed
and will feast forever
on trilliums and tulips

if I choose to stay my foot.

I don't, but stand a moment musing,
their sticky deaths the mucilage
holding me earthbound
by all that is at once

most vulnerable
most destructive.

ALBINO RAINBOWS

White, they ought not to exist.
— One in a thousand, ladies and gentlemen —

> Our heels hammer the iron catwalks
> between gray concrete tanks
> like submerged bunkers.

— Of these, few live.
Hawks can spot them
from a mile up.
Their own prey
sees them and hides.
They go hungry —

> These, then, are miracles.
> Long, pale as my arm.
> Color of nail parings
> or dissolving newsprint.
> Gills yellowish,
> grimy tavern windows through which
> the pink blood flashes
> its slow, smudged neon.
> They wear red goggles
> as if in a darkroom.
> Their mouths seep blood at the corners.

— Like mules, friends,
almost invariably
sterile —

> Magic bullets in the black
> racing heart of the water.
> Silver rockets that never
> arrive. The radio silent,
> spilled water dancing
> like mercury in the airless cabin.

— unusually big.
We feed them well.
Still they grow
very slowly —

        Plump and flaccid as rising loaves,
        hanging listless among the bubbles
        from the hiccuping aerator.

— largest collection anywhere.
For the medical school.
No, I don't know exactly —

        A handful of grain,
        a dingy spiral nebula.
        Our heels make hollow carnival.

— One in a thousand —

THE BICENTENNIAL CIRCUS

Comfortably cross-legged, Betsy Ross is sewing.
Her mobcap is made of diamonds. From her lap
a fiery spill of sequined stars and stripes
expands to drape her homespun elephant.

Behind ride half a hundred beauties. Each
sports a tricolor tail of plumes propped wide
on giant popsicle sticks. Each coyly perches
sidesaddle, and from her wrinkled beast, blows kisses.

Don't tread on me. The mammoth hooves pound
like mortars through the swirl of roustabouts,
mahouts, and aerialists. Here's dwarf Ben Franklin,
kite bobbing near the knees of Uncle Sam
on stilts. Spotlights electrify them both.

From Bulgaria, a literal family tree.
This year a new machine, half pendulum,
half catapult, will launch them in pairs, then singly
on wobbly somersaults through the loud air,
to land astonished on each other's shoulders,
their leapfrog couplings, piled-on pyramids
a sweaty burlesque of genealogy.

The animal trainer's costumed as Spartacus.
A metal comb surmounts his slit-eyed casque.
His beer-hall gut is swathed in silver gauze,
his shins in chain mail puttees. At his command
the somnolent lions roll over and play live.

The bicentennial circus! The parents are on their feet
and they're cheering! Jaded voyagers adrift
through seas of spilled coke, archipelagoes
of popcorn, this parade's their fabled Indies,
rank and alluring.

A lesser landfall lies
beyond the fulminating spotlight where,
in unpatriotic black and gold, the tigers
pace and return in their stroboscopic cages.

RAIN

Rain is the original stereotype,
billions of identical units, each intent
on the din of its own tiny bit of information
about ice crystals, say, at forty thousand feet,
wind shear, or the pollen count
on the Siberian tundra.

It begins like a sprung nerve, twitching.
An invisible junco lands
on the laurel, then a flock of them.
Something plays the ferns like a marimba.
It continues, in Satie's directions, *monotonously, whitely —
like a nightingale with a toothache.*
But this is more accurately rodent weather:
a clatter of nails and tail-tips on roof and walls,
the sour smell of a sickroom,
fear of bites while sleeping.

Awake and needing something I go downtown.
Rain draws the maimed in thunderous masses
out into the slick streets as if to a shrine.
The dwarfs, the obese, the amputees, the mumblers, the dropsical
old women whose feet would make fine umbrella stands
crowd stupefied beneath the gray fountain
to be healed or drown,
and my taxi driver, taking a wrong turn, asks "Lady
why do you look so sad?

You must be some kind of artist."

PROTEUS

My master liked to play tricks. He'd toss
a shaggy blue paw at the shore
and when he jerked it back like a clumsy conjuror
there'd be mullet jumping, or a ransom
of unspent agates, gone with the next wave.
Little things.
No matter how hard he tried
his heart was too vast, liquid and cold
to cram into one body.
I'm more volatile. I think now he told me
what to do out of jealousy.

Like any craft, it was hurtful and crude at first.
How I struggled to throw the combers on, a pelt
that seldom fit.
I blush to recall my juvenilia:
the three-legged bears, the tailless crocodiles.
My audience didn't notice.
Even then they complained I didn't communicate
though the tongues of my whole zoo rattled like clappers,
though by then I had perfected
all my little tricks of dentition
and my bones — this is prophetic! — functioned like slide rules.

Just when I got things right, they said I'd retired.
But I went where the work was.
The modern world offers too many theatres.
The price of art is anonymity.
Nobody recognizes the aberrant blip on the oscilloscope,
the unexplained ghost on the late show,
the alarm in the peaceful house.
The times are against me: consider
those cereals more permanent than marble.

The work now is sterile,
exhausting, all bit parts and banality,
those hideous lives of agar and centrifuge,
as if simple replication were ever enough!
I'm a classicist. I liked
roles I could sink my teeth into.
And only my vacations, being sunlight
on a Dutch wall, or a hatch of Monarch butterflies
by an abandoned railhead, have kept me
— I can't say whole — but going.

I'm at the top, now, of my forms
and I'm staying put.
I am anything I choose
though you're too slow to follow
while I run through all my frequencies, visible, invisible
with the rippling grace of a dancer at the barre.
Virtuosity has its hazards. Faster! Faster!
My sine waves snap and hum like rubber bands.
My peacocks and my coelacanths melt together
into that gray, bureaucratic blur your dull eyes,
beating twelve plodding times per minute,
mistake for normal
mistake for yourself.

But I know, I warn you, where I am going
and my great speed steadies me.

MIDAS

The despicable elements of his life survived,
the ones he either couldn't touch or wouldn't:
scullions, major-domos, plenipotentiaries
back from alarming embassies; seneschals
and huntsmen, farriers, furriers, and seamstresses;
charwomen, varlets, helots, his prime minister,
a sorcerer or two, and the palace dwarf.

The first few were marvels. His favorite cook, for example,
bent double beneath a boar's head surrounded by thrushes,
the platter alone worth a year of barbarian revenues
(he'd had the bad luck to wobble); not to mention
the exquisite verisimilitude of the notched
birds' tongues, the boar's splintered tusks, the pucker, swell,
and ooze of the gold-leaf burn on the cook's right thumb.
Then came a gardener, toothless, offering pears,
the queen (she'd grabbed at a pear), and his old nurse
with perfect gadroon borders of tears down both
sides of her nose (he'd thoughtlessly wiped one away).

The later groups were hilarious. He'd thought
it wise at first to have them all stacked in the treasury
to be melted down in case of war or inflation.
By then, of course, the able-bodied were mostly
frozen, golden. Urging on the stumblers
he'd lost, or gained, a number of them forever.
There was, in addition, an excessively numerous
but touching family group, come to retrieve
a son for burial, but whether out of grief
or avarice, he would never know for sure.

Then it got worse. He passed through hunger and thirst
to permanent horniness. Loneliness was the worst.
The few survivors gibbered at him from galleries
and antechambers. Above the chatter of metal
leaves, and the ripe grapes chiming like little bells
from the arbors, he could hear the elusive whisper
of clothing, flesh. Each silken or raucous voice was a siren's.

Then he thought of the ones he'd lugged off and hidden himself:
the golden girls in pornographic poses,
the boys with polished Hesperidean backsides,
— even a cunning goat with lost-wax curls.
He had draped them all in out-of-season tunics.
His lust and shame made monumental sculpture.

And now, you think, it's time for the happy ending.
But Dionysus begs off. He's no soft touch,
for flesh once lost to art is lost for good.
We leave the king forever as we found him,
in the rich glare of his punishment, dazzled to blindness
by appetites he can neither hide nor die of.

THE LINGUISTIC COMMISSION REPORTS FROM THE INTERIOR

Unlike our country, where the words
are small, succulent and docile
theirs, wiry and mean,
must be cornered and battered with rocks.
Even then they may break loose, snapping and foaming.
Their least bite can fester.

The adverbs are especially menacing.
They circle the tents at night,
making sleep impossible
though hammocks help a little.

The nouns, nocturnal and clumsy,
are sluggish by day, hence
easily ambushed. In
captivity they breed copiously:
five hundred variants of "want,"
a thousand nuances of "hunger,"
each stringy, foul-tasting.

Small wonder the natives chew air
constantly to numb the pain,
washing it down with a brew of stinging
nettles that resembles *pulque;*

or that they cruelly cast out to die
old orations, epigrams, homilies
— even the small-beer mutterings
and yelps of love —
though they might, with care, have lasted centuries;

or that their most sacred object
is a blank piece of paper,
their epic poem
seventeen hours of silence,
their highest virtue panic
in the face of hyperbole.

47

AFTER *APPALACHIAN SPRING*

I

With song and blessing
they have linked arms and walked
a while together, finding
a home in the warm instant.

And now the parson strides out into the night
those four foolish virgins,
his followers, a fluttering
kite tail behind him.
But from some space
in back of the broadbrimmed moon
they watch, a constellation in the mind.

In the still house
lamplight and dying firelight
flow together like fresh and salt water,
and the lovers drift
at the surface of sleep
bubbling imaginary kisses.

The flared sleeves and skirt
of the pioneer woman's dress
have made of her closet
a small carillon.
In a few hours, refreshed,
she will step out in the wide dawn
and with measured stride
set a new day ringing.

II

Led, wheeled, or carried — we are not to know —
in flamboyant red and purple chiffon caftan,
in gold orthopedic shoes deliberately like buskins,
the black chignon as big and rare as a roc's egg,
belladonna eyes, and wattles daubed with carmine,
she confronts us like a siege engine.

We are one vast, slovenly, panting creature.
Black head, red body,
she jerks the breath from our throats,
drinks us in little sips.
She is distant, minute, gorged
as the curtain slaps down.

AT THE PIANO

I

Hunchback
minotaur
squared off
on black goat feet
tight-lipped, eyeless, mute
you are cornered.
Now
I will fold you back like a quilt.
You will grin
like a glad foolish hound.
At my touch
your hollow flank
will buzz like a great golden hive
and the stinging
swarms rush out
singing their unknown language.

II

The keys rise to my fingers
            like diving boards
            like the pliant stems of flowers
            like necks bared to the axe
            like the stairways of crumbling cities
            like masses of candelabra
            like the pits of ripe fruit.

They frolic like minnows.
They lie down like mild lambs.
They arch their necks like zebras.
They snap their beaks like macaws.

They are ponderous as the elephant
delicate as the garter snake
furious as the black swan.

I rejoice in their many lives.
We are one, well-knit
as a barrel stave,
the perfect, gravity-defying round
through which the sun leaps.

A MUSICAL OFFERING

For Marvin Mc Gee

I

At Christmas, your telegram:
*I love you. I've lost
your telephone number.* No one
else gives me such presents, although
I can't remember now
what, when I called you, we said.

II

*The nearer I came to my native city, the more frequent
were the letters from my father. I therefore hurried forward
as fast as I could, although myself far from well.
My mother's disease was consumption. Seven weeks ago she died.
Ah, who was happier than I when I could still
utter the sweet name, mother, and it was heard?
And to whom can I say it now?*
                              *I have passed
very few pleasant hours since my arrival here.
To the asthma which I fear may develop
into consumption is added melancholy
as great an evil as my malady itself.
In Augsburg you lent me three carolins, but I
must entreat for a time your indulgence.
My journey cost me a great deal, and I have not
the smallest hopes of earning anything here.
Fate is not propitious to me here in Bonn.
Pardon my chatter; it was necessary
for my justification.*
                    *I am, with the greatest respect,
Your most obedient servant and friend —*
                                        Here,
on page eighty-nine, sunk in my own life,
I abandoned Beethoven, and since have read no further,
nor played his music, nor written to you.

52

III

In the dark house all that remains
is a gas log on the stone hearth
two brass urns in leaded window niches
through which the blue day shines
and a grand piano.
                        A girl raises the lid
sits down and plays
a Bach partita. There is pure, airborne order.
The room lights up with blue butterflies.

A moment only. Her fingers stammer and stop.
The wings clap shut. The thread of music snaps.
Patiently she goes back, repeats, pieces together
the broken ends. There is a way out
of the dark house. She must have the wit to play it.

IV

Last year I sent my piano,
older than I, younger
by far than you, away to be rebuilt.
Where it stood, the percussion marks
of my pedal heel overlapped
like ragged valves, at the top
of a lopsided heart outlined in yellow varnish.

Pianos age as we do.
The soundboard, that heartwood
dries with time into its glory.
Cellulose, lignin, its ranks
of vegetable pipes hum at the least touch.

But the metal plate, under tons
of deep-sea pressure, buckles
and sags like a sunk galleon.
The rigged strings go slack.
Bits of wire and felt
sprout like hair in odd places.
The machine, in short, decays. The singing voice
falters, damped by excessive tolerances.

Now, what a comeback! Copper strings like store teeth,
a giant clipspring bolted into the belly,
(that curve more tender than any living flank),
and the huge shifty voice of a ventriloquist.

My cyborg, my pony, I don't know you,
with your face-lift and your megaphone, mysterious
like all my old friends.

V

Heartbroken when the Great War began
old La Pérouse stopped eating. Gide found his piano teacher
in a threadbare velvet armchair, not wanting to die
in the bed he shared with his termagant wife. The shutters
were almost closed. Imagine that dark room
with its senile clutter: a pile of hatboxes;
a bureau covered with uncut books; a garbage can
full of worn-out shoes; a dozen spirit lamps,
lit and unlit, like random votive lights;
untouched glasses of cider, and flies circling
loud in the August heat. The old man's face
was parchment white, spattered with the confetti
of age, fever, chagrin. Picture his mouth,
flabby and toothless, working its cud of grief.

Gide slipped him swallows of cider and sips of broth
each time he paused between injuries. Then he eased him
to his feet, found his hat, and helped him downstairs.

So the man who had written *The Immoralist*
and the old musician went their ways, La Pérouse
to his café, while Gide, unable to write,
played Bach all day, "preferring," he noted later,
"the fugues with a joyful rhythm," though the war went on.

Retelling this fable, I think of you and am comforted.

VI

Old man, I beg you, do not
die yet. Teach me again
the art of things done badly
for love.

THE PRICE OF ADMISSION

He is a toll taker in a temple of art.
He measures the passage of time by the price of admission,
twice now what it was when he first entered
his glass kiosque, half orgone box, half telephone booth.

More people took taxis then. In the sculpture garden
the ruminant bronze nudes caught the light
and tossed it back all day, exact change.
The soul of a petty bureaucrat . . . he has grown a mustache
above his tamed mouth, and wears
the visor of his cap pulled down hard.
But sometimes he catches his own panicky eyes
peering back from the glass surround, the eyes of a man
caught forever in a revolving door.

At night, acid and the meticulous burin.
Its handle fits his palm like a ticket punch.
On the veins and scars of the zinc plate, his eyeshade
casts the green light of an unattainable forest.
Sylvan, sylvan . . . again the child is crying
whom they named for two great saints of Russian literature,
and his thin wife pushes her food away uneaten.

The sculpture garden has shrunk to the length of a boxcar.
In it the plump Maillols huddle like refugees
and the sun sifts down in ashes.
                              After the fire
the empty charred frames went out like coffins,
a bearer at each gilt corner.
Once it cost only a dollar to enter.
He was young, about to be famous.
Above him, invisible,
were Giacomettis slim as little goats
and the water lilies' unblemished platters of light.

THE TEN THOUSANDTH NIGHT

Prince, this is my last story. Listen
to the din that screams through clenched teeth into your ears.
Feel the hot grit scour your eyelids, and the force
that lifts and whirls you through thinnest air to the uttermost
edge of the world, effacing all inscriptions,
as the djinn's furious breath sputters and stops.

This is the last oasis. An obsequious vapor
hovers above the sandstone spines of palm trees
and their hacked, bedraggled foliage. Restless among them,
behind them, grimy silhouettes you guess
as camels, cattle, hinds, black goats, pass
and repass, their fabulous colors crushed to dun.

The hidden water jangles like a miser's purse,
and you enter the last palace. Erected this instant,
or coalesced, it has been here always, crumbling,
or heaped up again, a dune formalized.
Pass, prince, through the intricate portals that clamp shut
as the glittering passages pale and narrow, while
the dust you walk turns ever whiter and finer,
desert skin no sun touches.

Now gloat over your last treasures: corroded chests
brimming with the mild rainbow eyes of victims,
the stolen glare of diamonds; and lamps to whose spouts
you lean without touching, listening
for the voices of murderous wind, and the vast
conspiracies of shipwreck. Scuttle over this wealth
and fall, drowned and gasping, into the final

room. You are marooned in hollow glory
carved by a giant tongue. The grandiose spiral
of your life narrows to thirst. Before you, veiled

the last woman waits, salt-white, wavering,
a fountain of tears grown old beyond all fiction.
And now the clever hasps of her heart spring open.
My lord, you are enthroned there, tiny, gorgeous,
expectant.
                   But I have lost all my voices,
however many dog-eared nights remain.
Prince, it has always been the same story
and always it ends in death.

NOTES

"The Hour-glass." The title and the italicized quotations are from *The Journal of Jules Renard,* translated by Louise Bogan and Elizabeth Roget (New York: George Braziller, 1964).

"Mare's Milk." An impersonation loosely based on incidents and quotations from the Tolstoys' letters and journals, which I have taken from Henri Troyat's *Tolstoy* (New York: Doubleday, 1967).

"Edith Ascending" and "Edith Cast Down." These two poems owe their existence to R. W. B. Lewis's *Edith Wharton: A Biography* (New York: Harper & Row, 1975). The narrator of the first poem is an imaginary monk at the Franciscan monastery of La Verna, which Edith Wharton and Walter Berry visited during the summer of 1912. The voice of the second poem purports to be Edith Wharton's own just before her death in August 1937.

"Dread." A mastiff named Dread was one of the subjects of Eadweard Muybridge's photographic studies of animal locomotion.

"Proteus." Defined in Webster's *New International Dictionary,* second edition, as "a prophetic sea-god in the service of Poseidon (Neptune). When seized, he would assume different shapes, so trying to escape prophesying. Hence, one who easily changes his appearance or principles."

"After *Appalachian Spring.*" The dance choreographed by Martha Graham to the music of Aaron Copland.

"A Musical Offering." The second section is freely condensed and paraphrased from Beethoven's letter to Dr. Schaden, written from Bonn, September 15, 1787, quoted in *Thayer's Life of Beethoven,* revised and edited by Elliot Forbes (Princeton: Princeton University Press, 1967). The incidents of section V are from volume 1 of *The Journals of André Gide,* translated, selected, and edited by Justin O'Brien (New York: Vintage Books, 1959).

"The Price of Admission." One of Monet's great series of water-lily paintings was completely destroyed in the fire at the Museum of Modern Art, New York, in 1958.

PITT POETRY SERIES

Ed Ochester, General Editor

Milne Holton and Paul Vangelisti, eds., *The New Polish Poetry: A Bilingual Collection*

David Huddle, *Paper Boy*

Shirley Kaufman, *The Floor Keeps Turning*

Shirley Kaufman, *From One Life to Another*

Shirley Kaufman, *Gold Country*

Abba Kovner, *A Canopy in the Desert: Selected Poems*

Paul-Marie Lapointe, *The Terror of the Snows: Selected Poems*

Larry Levis, *Wrecking Crew*

Jim Lindsey, *In Lieu of Mecca*

Tom Lowenstein, tr., *Eskimo Poems from Canada and Greenland*

Archibald MacLeish, *The Great American Fourth of July Parade*

Peter Meinke, *The Night Train and The Golden Bird*

James Moore, *The New Body*

Carol Muske, *Camouflage*

Gregory Pape, *Border Crossings*

Thomas Rabbitt, *Exile*

Belle Randall, *101 Different Ways of Playing Solitaire and Other Poems*

Ed Roberson, *Etai-Eken*

Ed Roberson, *When Thy King Is A Boy*

Eugene Ruggles, *The Lifeguard in the Snow*

Dennis Scott, *Uncle Time*

Herbert Scott, *Groceries*

Richard Shelton, *The Bus to Veracruz*

Richard Shelton, *Of All the Dirty Words*

Richard Shelton, *The Tattooed Desert*

Richard Shelton, *You Can't Have Everything*

Gary Soto, *The Elements of San Joaquin*

Gary Soto, *The Tale of Sunlight*

David Steingass, *American Handbook*

David Steingass, *Body Compass*

Tomas Tranströmer, *Windows & Stones: Selected Poems*

Alberta T. Turner, *Learning to Count*

Alberta T. Turner, *Lid and Spoon*

Marc Weber, *48 Small Poems*

David P. Young, *Sweating Out the Winter*